Speaking and Listening

Cats, Hats and Hippos

Ruth Thomson
and Pie Corbett

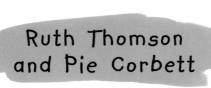

Chrysalis Children's Books

First published in the UK in 2004 by
Chrysalis Children's Books an imprint of
Chrysalis Books Group plc
The Chrysalis Building,
Bramley Road, London, W10 6SP

© Chrysalis Books Group plc 2004
Text © Ruth Thomson and Pie Corbett
Illustrations © Chrysalis Books Group plc 2003

ISBN 1 84458 037 7

British Library Cataloguing in Publication Data
for this book is available from the British Library.

Editorial manager: Joyce Bentley
Editor: Nicola Edwards
Designers: Rachel Hamdi, Holly Mann
Illustrators: Sofie Forrester, Kevin McAleenan,
Joanna Partis and Lucy Richards

Printed in China

Contents

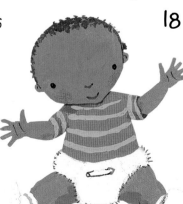

Speaking and listening

Talking helps children to think and to communicate, and to make sense of the world around them. Children's speech flourishes where there are interesting activities to talk about. This happens through play, discussing what is happening around them, looking at interesting objects and books and talking about what has happened at home or in school.

Telling the story of what the family or class has done and inventing stories together are helpful ways to develop talk and the imagination. Saying funny sentences, inventing rhymes and singing are also important.

> I spy with my little eye a butterfly and an apple pie.

About this book

This book is designed for adults (whether parents, carers or teachers) and children to talk about together. It is brimming with activities that will give children opportunities to talk out loud, to develop their abilities to speak in a wide variety of ways and to listen carefully.

The activities

Each double page has a particular focus (see the contents page) and is completely self-contained. You can open the book at any page, talk together about what you see in the detailed pictures and go backwards or forwards at whim.

However, although the book has no fixed order, the activities in the first half are simpler than those in the second half. The early pages encourage children to say one particular sound or word, to make rhymes or reply to simple questions. Later pages stimulate children to respond at greater length to the pictures or to make up simple stories.

You do not need to do all the activities on each page at one sitting – the book has been deliberately designed to be re-read again and again, with more things to discover at each re-reading.

Extension activities

There are further suggestions for each theme on pages 30 and 31. These, in turn, may prompt you to invent more activities of your own.

Talking and listening guidelines

There are suggested guidelines for how good speakers and listeners behave on page 32.

How to use this book

The four activities on each double page provide starting points for conversation. Some invite children to discuss what they see, suggest ideas and use talk in an exploratory way. Others may require a more formal response, using particular sentences and vocabulary. In some cases, sentence openers or models are given in bold print. These are suggestions for developing different types of sentence or vocabulary, eg positional language or the use of complex sentences, which may help children take their first steps into developing talk beyond one or two word comments. You could also lead from a talking session into writing.

Responses

The pictures have been drawn so that there are usually many different possible responses – since an atmosphere of 'getting it right or wrong' will not encourage children to speak up. Children talk best when they feel relaxed and people around them are interested in what they have to say. If children seem uncertain, begin by modelling a sentence structure. If a child's reply misses a word or lacks clarity, repeat a clear version.

Copycat

The children could also play *Copycat*, repeating sentences that you have just said. Use a glove puppet to make this game more fun. Ask a question to which the puppet replies. The children then imitate the puppet. After you have modelled a few replies, the children can think of a reply for themselves, rehearse it in pairs and say it aloud to the class.

a warm-up task, encouraging close observation of the picture

a list of useful words

the focus of the talking activity

the talking activity you ask the child to do

a sample answer

the sentence structure to encourage the child to use

Sounds all around

Say the sounds.

★ **Tell me**

Tell me what the different characters are doing.

◌ The baby is crying.

◌ The dog is asleep.

★ **Say beginning sounds**

Choose a sound, eg **m-** (look at the list).

What can you see that begins with **m-**?

◌ **m**an, **m**op, **m**at, **m**ug, **m**um

Some beginning sounds

b- (as in **b**ag)
c- (as in **c**ot)
ch- (as in **ch**in)
d- (as in **d**ad)
e- (as in **e**gg)
f- (as in **f**ish)
h- (as in **h**am)
j- (as in **j**am)
l- (as in **l**id)
m- (as in **m**at)
n- (as in **n**et)
p- (as in **p**en)
r- (as in **r**ug)
s- (as in **s**ock)
sh- (as in **sh**eep)
t- (as in **t**ap)
v- (as in **v**an)
w- (as in **w**eb)
z- (as in **z**oo)

Some end sounds

-am (as in h**am**)
-an (as in m**an**)
-ap (as in t**ap**)
-at (as in c**at**)
-ck (as in so**ck**)
-ed (as in r**ed**)
-eg (as in l**eg**)
-en (as in h**en**)
-id (as in l**id**)
-ig (as in p**ig**)
-in (as in b**in**)
-ip (as in z**ip**)
-ish (as in d**ish**)
-op (as in m**op**)
-ot (as in c**ot**)
-ox (as in b**ox**)
-ug (as in j**ug**)
-um (as in dr**um**)
-ut (as in n**ut**)

★ **Say end sounds**

Choose an end sound, eg **–am** (look at the list).

What can you see that ends with **–am**?

◯ h**am**, r**am**, j**am**

★ **Say the rhyming word**

Pick an object, eg **cat**.

Can you find something that rhymes with it?

◯ **H**at rhymes with **cat**.

Rhyme time

Make some rhymes.

On the rug, I saw...

a jug   a mug   a dog   a slug

In a van, I saw...

a man   a pin   a pan   a fan

Under a log, I saw...

a dog   a frog   a flag   a cog

In the den, I saw...

some men   a pen   a hen   a bun

★ **Spot the odd one out**

Choose a line of pictures. Say the words.
Which is the odd one out?

○ R**ug**, j**ug**, m**ug**, d**og**, sl**ug**.
D**og** is the odd one out.

★ **Finish the rhyme**

Choose a line of pictures. Pick a word
to finish the rhyme.

○ On the r**ug**, I saw a sl**ug**.
○ Through the g**ap**, I saw a m**ap**.

Beside the rock, I saw...

a clock   a cock   a duck   a sock

Under the mat, I saw...

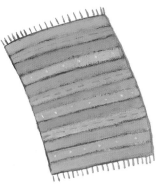   

a cot   a cat   a bat   a hat

Through the gap, I saw...

  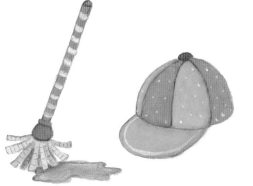 

a dog nap   a mop   a cap   a map

Out at sea, I saw...

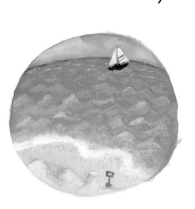    

a tree   a bee   a tray   a key

★ **Do the words rhyme?**

Choose a pair of words, eg **pen** and **hen** or **map** and **mop**. Do they rhyme?

🗨 **Pen** and **hen** rhyme. **Map** and **mop** don't rhyme.

★ **Make up your own rhymes**

Use the rhyming words to invent your own rhymes. Can you think of any more rhyming words?

🗨 A **bee** buzzed round a **tree**, looking for a **flea**.

Who's at the door?
Play some alphabet games.

★ **Who's there?**
Choose a door. Say the sound of the letter on it.
Make up a name for the character that begins
with the same sound.

💬 **V**anessa the **v**iolinist

★ **Say the sounds**
Choose a door. Say the sound of the letter on it,
eg **n-**. What can you see that begins or ends
with that sound?

💬 **n**urse, **n**eck, **n**ose, **n**ewspaper, **n**otebook

★ **Say a silly sentence**

Choose a letter. Invent a silly sentence
using as many words beginning with the
same sound as possible.

🗩 **N**ora the **n**osy **n**urse **n**eeds **n**ewspapers at **n**ight.

★ **Play the alphabet game**

Take turns to add a new character
to an alphabetical list.

🗩 **I opened the door and saw** an **a**stronaut.

I opened the door and saw an **a**stronaut and a **b**oy.

pick a pair

Talk about everyday things.

★ **Tell me**

Choose an object. Say what you know about it.
What is it? What is it like? How do you use it?

💬 **This is a** hairbrush. **It has** a handle and lots
of bristles. **You use it to** brush your hair.

★ **What's this?**

Give some clues about an object, eg a hat,
for someone else to guess what it is.

💬 **This is** soft and stripy. **It has** a bobble.
You wear it on your head.

★ **Why do they go together?**

Pick an object. Find its partner.

Say why the two things go together.

💬 The bucket and spade **go together because** you play with them on the beach.

★ **Pair them up**

Find pairs of things that have either the same use, colour, shape, texture or material.

Say why they go together.

💬 The cup and the bucket both hold water.

13

Bird spotting
Describe these birds.

★ **Tell me**

Describe one of the birds. What colour is it? What is it doing?

💬 **I can see** a blue bird, standing with a long worm in its mouth.

★ **Which way?**

Describe a bird by the direction in which it is looking or flying.

💬 **I can see** an orange bird flying **to the right**. **I can see** a green bird looking **to the left**.

★ **Pick a pair**

Describe a pair of birds for someone
else to find.

💬 **Can you find** two blue birds pecking for food?
Can you find two green flying birds?

★ **Describe the differences**

Choose any two birds. Say what is the same
about them and what is different.

💬 **These birds are both** orange. **One is** flying
upwards and **the other is** flying downwards.

15

When the wind blew
Spot the changes.

★ **Tell me**

Choose some people. Say where they are and what they are doing.

◯ **I can see** a lady on a balcony watering some flowers.

★ **Ask some questions**

Take turns to ask a question about the picture. Use words such as **Who? What? Where? Why?**

◯ **What** colour is the flag?

◯ **Who** has got a dog?

★ **What has changed?**

Describe what happened when the wind blew.

💬 **When the wind blew,** the flowerpots fell off the balcony. Some of them smashed. One of them landed on the dog's head.

★ **How does everyone feel?**

Describe how the people in one of the pictures feel and why.

💬 The street sweeper is cross, **because** the wind has blown away his pile of leaves.

17

Growing up

Say what babies and children do.

★ **Tell me**

Use the pictures to help you describe what babies do.

🗨 Babies sleep a lot and drink milk.

★ **When you were a baby**

Describe what you did as a baby.

🗨 **When I was a baby, I** slept in a cot and wore nappies.

★ **Now you're older**

Say what you do now.

💬 **Now I'm older, I** sleep in a bed and dress myself.

★ **Talk about your day**

Use the pictures to describe your day from start to finish.

💬 **First of all**, I get out of bed. **Then** I go to the loo. **Next**, I get dressed. **After that**, I have breakfast...

Where are the animals?
Find the animals on the ark.

★ **Tell me**

Choose an animal. Say what it is and some things you know about it.

◯ **This is** an elephant. **It's** very big **and has** large ears and a long trunk.

★ **Where is each animal?**

Use the list of position words to describe where the animals are on the ark.

◯ The bear is **behind** the elephant.

◯ The dolphin is **in** the sea.

Useful position words

above
across
against
alongside
around
behind
below
beneath
beside
between
down
in
in front of
inside
into
near
next to
on
on top of
out of
over
through
under
underneath
up
with

★ **Ask questions**

Take turns to ask a question about where the animals are.

○ **Which animal is between** a hippo and a lion?

★ **Give a clue**

Explain where an animal is, eg the monkey, without naming it. Can someone else say what it is?

○ **This animal is climbing up** the flagpole.

How do you do it?

Making a jam sandwich

Getting dressed

★ **Tell Them**

Tell the robots what they need for an activity.

◯ **To make** a jam sandwich, **you need** bread, butter, jam...

★ **Step by step**

Choose an activity. Tell the robots what to do, step by step.

◯ **First** put the bread on the bread board. **Then** cut two slices with the bread knife. **Next... Finally...**

Wrapping a present

Planting a seed

★ **What has the silly robot done?**
The silly robot does everything wrong.
Say what it has done.
○ **The silly robot has** dropped all the seeds.

★ **Give instructions**
List the things that the robots will need for other everyday activities, eg going swimming or having a bath. Give them instructions on what to do.

Whose is this?
Talk about these people.

★ **Tell me**

Tell me three things about a character.

💬 *The knight wears armour. He carries a shield. He lives in a castle.*

★ **Make the link**

What has each character lost?

Match the objects to their owners.

💬 **The** doctor **has lost** her stethoscope.

★ **Making sentences**

Make up a funny sentence about
a character and an object.

◯ *The pirate tripped over a football.*

★ **Imagine a conversation**

Choose two characters. What might they say?

◯ *The queen said to the doctor, "My head hurts."*

◯ *The doctor replied, "Your crown is too heavy."*

What's happening here?

Describe what is going on.

★ **Tell me**

Choose a picture. Say what's happening in it.

◌ There are two people in a boat that is about to sink. Hungry crocodiles are swimming around them...

★ **What do they say?**

Imagine what the people in one of the pictures might be saying to one another.

◌ "Can you see anything in the cave?"

◌ "There's a big pair of eyes."

★ **What will happen next?**

Choose a picture. Say what you think might happen next.

◯ The family decide to creep into the cave. A fierce dragon is waiting for them. It...

★ **Tell the tale**

Make up a whole story about one of the pictures. Give each character a name. Describe where the story is set.

◯ Once there were two children called...

A story map
Make up your own story.

★ **Begin your story**

Choose one or two of the characters. Give them names. Decide who they are going to visit and where this person lives.

💬 **Once upon a time**, (names) **set off to visit** (a person) **who lived in** (a place).

★ **What did they find?**

Choose a path for your characters to take. What magic object do they find on it?

💬 **They took the path** up the mountain. **On their way, they found...** What do they do with it?

★ **What goes wrong?**

Who is blocking their path?

What surprising thing happens?

💬 **Suddenly, they met a... who...**

What do your characters say and do?

★ **What happens next?**

How do the characters use the magic object to help them? What happens next? Where do they go? How does your story end?

💬 The giant chased after them, but they jumped onto the magic carpet and...

Extension activities

Pages 6-7   Sounds all around

This double spread provides practice in hearing the sounds at the start and end of words.

★ Invent alliterative sentences for the child to finish, eg **T**eeny **T**om **t**apped. . . (his **t**ummy, a **t**in, the **t**able, a **t**ambourine); **B**ossy **B**etty **b**ought a **b**ig...

★ Point to an object. Ask the child to say what it is and then to find another object that begins with the same sound, eg **d**og and **d**oll or **b**ag and **b**all.

★ Play *I-spy*. Choose an object in the picture and say, I can see something beginning with... The child has to guess what it is.

Pages 8-9   Rhyme time

These two pages provide practice in hearing the sounds at the end of words and making rhymes.

★ Choose a word, eg **cat**. Take it in turns to say a word that rhymes with this (including nonsense words), until no-one can think of any more, eg **fat, splat, rat, drat, gnat**, etc. Simple rhyming endings with lots of words include: **-ack, -ame, -ay, -eet, -ell, -et, -id, -ill, -in, -ip, -ock, -ole, -ot, -un**.

★ Say some simple phrases, eg a **plate** in a **crate** or a **mole** in a **net**, for the child to say whether the words rhyme or not. If the words don't rhyme, ask the child to substitute a rhyming word.

★ Start some rhymes for the child to finish, eg My friend **Pete** likes eating...

Pages 10-11
Who's at the door?

This double spread concentrates upon sounds, letters and alphabetical order.

★ Play *The boy went shopping and bought...* Children think of words beginning only with **b** (eg **b**ottles, **b**ooks, **b**oots etc.) You could vary the game

(and the beginning sound) by choosing a pirate, cook or sailor instead.

★ Make up tongue twisters using the same beginning sound, eg **S**am the **s**illy **s**ailor **s**ells **s**ocks by the **s**ea.

★ Play *My cat*. Take turns to think of adjectives in alphabetical order, eg My cat is an **angry** cat. My cat is a **bad** cat. My cat is a **curious** cat.

Pages 12-13   Pick a pair

This double page is concerned with sorting and classifying objects in as many different ways as possible.

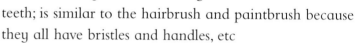
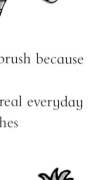

★ Choose an object. Ask children to link it to as many other things in the picture as possible, giving reasons, eg The toothbrush...is used with the toothpaste for cleaning teeth; is similar to the hairbrush and paintbrush because they all have bristles and handles, etc

★ Invent matching games. You could use real everyday objects, such as kitchen implements or clothes for children to categorise and match.

Pages 14-15   Bird spotting

These pages focus on precise description, categorising and identification and on learning directions.

★ Choose two birds side by side. Identify as many similarities and differences between them as possible – considering size, colour, activity, direction of flight, etc.

★ Compare and contrast. Use a collection of objects, such as buttons, coins or pictures on a theme, eg dogs, cut from magazines, to play similar matching games.

Pages 16-17   When the wind blew

The two pictures provide opportunities for making comparisons and showing cause and effect in sequence.

★ Ask children to describe the noises they might hear if this picture came alive, eg I can hear...the thud of the flower-pots, the flapping flag, the whistling wind, etc.

★ Ask children to describe *What happens when...* in all sorts of situations, eg when the traffic lights turn red, when you leave the bath tap running, etc.

Pages 18-19   Growing up

This double page offers opportunities for children to talk about themselves, their increasing achievements and their daily lives.

★ Using the pictures as prompts, talk about the sequence of changes in a baby's ability from birth to a toddler, and the things it needs and uses.

★ Talk about all the things the child can now do (that a baby can't) eg I can…ride a bike, hop on one leg, etc.

★ Introduce time vocabulary, eg **yesterday**, **today**, **next week**, **at the weekend**, **in the summer**, etc. Ask children to tell you a real or imaginary sequence of their activities for each time period.

Pages 20-21   Where are the animals?

The picture of the crowded ark is designed principally for practising prepositions (position words). However, it can also be used for talking about mathematical tasks, such as counting, sorting and matching.

★ **How many**… fish are there in the water? …animals are looking out of portholes? …are inside the cabin?

★ **Which animals**… can fly? …can swim? …have horns? …have wings? …have beaks? …have stripes?

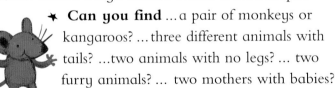

★ **Can you find** …a pair of monkeys or kangaroos? …three different animals with tails? …two animals with no legs? … two furry animals? … two mothers with babies?

Pages 22-23   How do you do it?

This double spread encourages children to use the appropriate conventions and language for giving instructions.

★ Play *Simon says*. Take it in turns to tell other players what to do, saying **Simon says**… at the start of each sentence, eg Simon says…Turn around… Shut your eyes, etc. Now and again, give an instruction *without* saying Simon says – and see if the other players still follow suit.

★ Give a set of instructions in the wrong order and ask children to put them in the right order. Use vocabulary such as **first**, **next** and **last** to encourage the sequencing.

Pages 24-25   Whose is this?

The pictures on this double spread can be used for activities such as describing, matching, making up sentences about characters and inventing conversations.

★ Use questions – **who, what, where, why, when, how** – to elicit more information about each character, eg **What** does the clown look like? **Where** is he throwing a custard pie? Encourage whole-sentence answers.

★ Ask children to link objects with people in other jobs or from well-known tales, such as: trowel - gardener; bowls of porridge - The Three Bears and Goldilocks, etc

Pages 26-27   What's happening here?

The four pictures each show an ambiguous situation, which children can interpret in as many imaginative ways as they like.

★ Play *Let's imagine*. Think of some other cliffhanger situations with alternative possible outcomes to talk about, such as a tiger escaping from a zoo, a dinosaur egg hatching at a museum, a toy coming to life, etc.

★ Jointly tell a story, taking turns to say a few sentences each, ending with a cliffhanger that the next person resolves before continuing the story, eg Once upon a time Jim went fishing. He soon felt a tug on the line. When he reeled it in, to his surprise, it was a…

Pages 28-29   Tell me a story

The story map offers alternative characters, routes and destinations to use in creating stories. Use traditional story language to help children structure their stories:

Openings: There was once… Long ago, there lived…

Build-ups: One day… Early one morning…

Problem: Suddenly… In an instant…All at once…

Resolution: So… When… As soon as…

Ending: In the end… At last… Finally…

Once children understand the structure of the story map, encourage them to use it as a basis for creating their own stories, using new characters, settings, magical objects and incidents.

How to be a good speaker and listener

When I speak, I need to:

★ Look at the person I'm talking to.

★ Make sure I say words clearly.

★ Speak loudly enough for everyone listening to hear me.

★ Ask questions about things I haven't understood.

★ Remember not to speak too fast.

★ Let other people join in and have a turn.

When I listen, I need to:

★ Look at the person who is speaking.

★ Keep still.

★ Follow carefully what the speaker is saying.

★ Wait until a speaker has finished before speaking.

★ Ask about anything I don't understand.

★ Give a reply if someone asks a question.